GREEK HISTORICAL WRITING

. AND

APOLLO

TWO LECTURES DELIVERED BEFORE
THE UNIVERSITY OF OXFORD
JUNE 3 AND 4, 1908

BY

ULRICH VON WILAMOWITZ-MOELLENDORFF

(*TRANSLATION BY GILBERT MURRAY*)

ARES PUBLISHERS INC.
CHICAGO   MCMLXXIX

Exact Reprint:
Oxford, 1908
ARES PUBLISHERS
612 N. Michigan Avenue
Chicago, Illinois 60611
Printed in the United States of America
International Standard Book Number
0-89005-320-0

ON GREEK HISTORICAL WRITING

WHEN I was trying to accustom myself to the thought of appearing for a few days in this unfamiliar world, I took it as a good omen that Magdalen College offered me hospitality; for a very famous Magdalen man has been an intimate friend of mine since my first years as a student. It is now forty years since I first acquired for my library, as my first book of learning in the English language, Edward Gibbon's immortal history. And now that I am here to expound to you my thoughts about the growth and the nature of historical writing in Greece, I gladly make Gibbon my starting-point.

Of course his work is admirable. Of course no Greek produced anything like it. And yet, if we apply to it the canon of historical research which the nineteenth century brought into vogue, it can only be called a work of research in the same qualified sense as the works of the ancients. Gibbon was no researcher in the strict sense. He made no inquiry into sources; he arrived at no new fact or datum. Despite all the labour he spent in reading his original authorities, despite all the freedom of his judgement, he walked in a prescribed path and he accepted a tradition. Without the laborious compilations which were achieved in the age of 'poly-history', without, for instance, the unsurpassable industry and learning of Tillemont, Gibbon's work would be unthinkable. What he does is, in essential, to give the traditional material shape by his literary art, and illuminate it with the enlightened intelligence of a man of the world who has assimilated all the culture of France and England. Different as is the temperament of the sarcastic unbeliever—' Gibbon's sneer,' as Lord Byron says—from the gentle piety of the Delphic priest, his method may be compared with that of Plutarch, whose *Lives* formed the favourite reading of the centuries between the Renaissance and the French Revolution. Plutarch also possessed great erudition ; but he owes the material of his narrative entirely to the historians and the Alexandrian compilers ; what he adds of his own is, apart from his charming presentation, only the criticism of a moralist and the political temper of the age of Trajan. Of course Plutarch was scarcely a historian, even in the ancient sense of the word. Yet even that fact has only been gradually recognized through the labours of the nineteenth century. To the Romans, Livy was without hesitation the historian κατ' ἐξοχήν. The history of the Republic was to them the same thing as Livy's narrative of it. In fact, what he says of his own feelings, and how his heart swells in writing of the ancient greatness of Rome which he depicts, holds good of his readers too. But the emotion is produced by the literary art of the rhetor and the tone of Augustan romanticism in which he writes. He accepted the tradition as he found it, and shaped it in this spirit not only without research but without any feeling for what we call historical truth.

We must always bear in mind that the ancients were even further from a genuine science of history than from a genuine science of nature. In that field where the eternal mistress, Nature, was always present, men succeeded much earlier in rising above the ancient limitations. The method of historical research which we regard as an imperative duty is scarcely a century old. Isolated individuals may have risen to its level before that, in both ancient and modern times ; but the general rule remains. And yet, even while we set ourselves to prove this from the development of historical writing in Greece, the first thing is to recognize that all our historical writing rests on foundations laid by the Greeks, as absolutely as does all our natural science.

Let us content ourselves with a hasty glance over the rest of the world. India shows us an Aryan people inferior to none in intellectual gifts, which, nevertheless, has remained altogether without history. At one moment, when Buddha, the founder of a new religion, gave the impulse, and his followers sought to preserve the incidents of his life, it seemed as if historical literature must come into being. But Buddha, too, soon entered into the realm of dateless myth. We need not doubt that the Teutons would have proved their ability to advance from the lays which contained their historical memories to real history ; but they did so in close dependence on the ancient tradition, which provided them not only with a fixed system of chronology in Jerome, but also with a universal history, if only in Orosius. Your great Beda belongs entirely to this line of development. And when in Germany individual men, like Otto von Frei-singen, really set themselves to depict contemporary history, they did so often in curiously close dependence on Sallust or Josephus. In Byzantium the thread of the tradition is unbroken ; there Herodotus and Thucydides were never lost to remembrance. Thousands of years before the Greeks, it is true, Egypt and Mesopotamia possessed records which amounted to a kind of chronicle, but the decisive step to a real historical literature seems never to have been taken there. The Old Testament, on the other hand, in many narratives—for instance in those of the reigns of David or Ahab, and earlier in the wonderful story of Abimelech in the *Book of Judges*— contains descriptions of a truth and fullness which no Greek has surpassed. It is possible enough that other Semites possessed some similar faculty. We find it in the Arabs immediately after Mohammed. The rebellion which cost the life of Othman, the third successor of the Prophet, is described to us more vividly than the murder of Caesar. And yet all the ancient Semites are lacking in exactly that quality through which the Greeks made the writing of history into a conscious art. They have historical writing, but they have no historian.

Hence it is that Herodotus is the father of history. How does he begin? '*This is Herodotus' account of what he has learnt by inquiry*'—of his '*Historië*.' His personality ultimately conditions what he describes. True, he announces his purpose, '*that Time may not destroy the remembrance of great deeds*'; and his main theme, '*the strife between barbarians and Greeks.*' But he proposes '*to wander through small and great cities in full knowledge that the lot of man has no permanence*'. Thus he leads us all over the world so far as he has seen it. There is nothing about the West, while he has made inquiries far and wide about the North and South. He delights also in reporting what he has been told; but that too is something that he has 'found out'. Even what he has taken from the written tradition has the same subjective air. In his rejection of all chronology he consciously sets himself in opposition to the impersonal chronicles, which he must have known. The political convictions of a determined democrat, the strange combination of *deisidaimonia* and rashness of criticism, imprints a subjective stamp on everything, except where the mere gossip lets himself go in sheer enjoyment of a good story.

The same subjectivity had already, in a few dry words, been recognized by Hecataeus as his guiding principle. But, as far as we know, he only narrated the heroic history. Certainly what Herodotus has to tell about Miletus points to a plain traditional chronicle of that place, nothing more ; and his account of the Ionian revolt does not come at all from Milesian information. Geography, indeed, in the wide sense which the Greeks always attached to the word, as comprising an abundance of historical material, owes its origin to the great commercial town of Miletus, just as Natural Science does ; and in this particular Herodotus is deeply indebted to Hecataeus. Nay, he has made considerable steps backward compared with him. But no Ionian can dispute with Herodotus the name of 'Father of History'.

Nevertheless, we must not put his image alone in the sanctuary which the 'Hero-founder' of history really deserves ; what belongs there is the double herm of the Naples Museum, which combines with Herodotus Thucydides. The one was a Halicarnassian of Carian and Dorian blood, of Ionian culture, and Athenian sympathies ; the other a half Thracian. Evidently, it is culture, not race, that is decisive. Herodotus and Thucydides combined : two men who complement one another, but as opposites ! The younger was fully conscious of this and made it clear in the superscription of his History : *Thucydides of Athens has described the war of the Peloponnesians and Athenians because he foresaw its incomparable importance.* Subjectivity is there sure enough ; the writer's own insight motives his choice of material, but this material has also its independent significance. The chronicler records that which happens because it happens ; he is, as it were, only a medium through which events fix themselves in writing. Hero-

dotus tells what he can and will ; what he tells and how
he tells it, depends upon his personality. Thucydides
reviews the mass of events and chooses by his own insight the part that is worthy of recital. This part he
undertakes to describe while it is actually happening ;
he works to that end and what lies outside his theme
does not interest him. Now this is a really scientific
procedure, and the first two were not. Thucydides also
speaks of his methods and his sources. His purpose is
by no means purely historical ; he explains that he
writes for the instruction of the statesmen of the future,
nay, he himself, when he began to write, expected to
pursue practical politics, and though this hope was not
fulfilled, he never quite throws off the statesman. Again
and again one is fain to compare him with Machiavelli. '
I need not waste words upon the great qualities of his
work ; his clearness and keenness of judgement never
fail him, not even when he treats the events of the past.
He enjoys destroying an historical fable by documentary
evidence. Still, his *Archaeologia* does not give an impres-
sion of personal research ; it gives only a rational criticism of accepted tradition. We may not ask for more ;
but also we should not discover more in it.

The influence of such a work must have been powerful. It is said that the minister of Dionysius the First,
Philistos, wrote a great work in the style of Thucydides ;
but we know no details. Xenophon, however, a man
very susceptible to stimulus from other minds, not only
attempted to complete the torso of Thucydides in his
own style, but actually did in the *Hellenica* write Thucydidean history, so far as he was able. We see indeed
that he is not master of his material, but is everywhere
hemmed in by the limits of his personal investigations
and the still narrower limits of his judgement ; but he

keeps up steadily the appearance of Thucydidean objectivity.

It is far more remarkable how the young Theopompus
in his *Hellenica* tried to steep himself entirely in the
spirit of Thucydides. We can now see this, thanks to
the Dioscuri of Queen's College, and it is a point of the
utmost importance. Theopompus's method of dividing
his matter, of representing the facts without ceremony,
and not only the events, but the motives of the persons
acting ; his habit of subjecting them all to criticism ;
his consequent pursuit of an objectivity which all the
while rests on a strong belief in his own superior insight—
all this is, or is meant to be, Thucydidean. And yet
the very different temperament of the writer, who is
not yet quite freely expressing his own nature, betrays
itself in his political judgements and also in a strain
of latent polemic. Theopompus, the Chian, had also
studied Herodotus and actually published an abridge-
ment of him. Like Thucydides, he was up to his old
age cut off from political activity. Like Herodotus, he
undertook great travels, whose results he wished like
him to turn to account. In Philip's empire-building he
found a worthy theme ; but even that did not content
him. He had made his own the fashionable arts of a
rhetoric which rivalled poetry ; and though he may well
have hated the philosophical ferment of the time, because
it was specifically Athenian, even his master Isocrates
represented certain moralizing tendencies ; he was
fascinated, too, by the magnificent daring of the grey-
haired Plato, who in his *Critias* had undertaken to represent in narrative fiction the ideal condition of human
society which he postulated as conceivable. Thus
Theopompus in the *Philippica* created a work which
contained more than the special merits of Herodotus

and Thucydides. The historico-political excursuses sub-
jected all the past to an uncompromising criticism from
the writer's own point of view, while the free fiction
of the *Meropis* challenged comparison with the Platonic
Utopias. It was in fact a work to which, as far as inten-
tion goes, I know no parallel in literature. It is impos-
sible to imagine what an influence such a book might
have exercised upon modern writing ; and it was actually
in existence in the ninth century. It must have lived
only to be burnt like so many others by the unsanctified
crusaders of Dandolo. The aim, of course, was too vast.
Theopompus wished to unite the fullness of the story-
teller Herodotus with the severity of the statesman
Thucydides, and at the same time to give speech to
his own thoughts, both in broad critical argumentation
and in the play of inventive fancy. Such a work was
no longer history ; but one might well call it *Historië*
raised to the nth power, a thing by itself, as is Plato's
trilogy—the *Republic, Timaeus, Critias.*

If I have made clear what Theopompus wished in
the *Philippica*, no word is needed to show the injustice
of his usual association with Ephorus, which, I regret
to say, I also for a long time accepted from the ancient
writers on rhetoric.   Ephorus, an utterly thoughtless
writer, has at best the doubtful merit of having been
the first to compose a Universal History, in the sense
in which that idea was developed afterwards. He
mastered a great mass of material, and, inasmuch as
he made it trivial, succeeded the better in making it
homogeneous. He 'pragmatized' history, as they call it ;
that is, he took care that everything should run on such
lines as an enlightened Philistine can at a pinch imagine.
He also took care that the moral and patriotic feelings of
the public should in the end receive the satisfaction which

they expect in the fifth act of a bad tragedy. Where
the tradition resisted, he brought it to reason with a
firm hand. We can be sure of our facts in this, because
just those parts of his work are specially well known to
us, in which he simply bases himself upon Herodotus and
Thucydides. There is nothing in them of any value,
except a few additional facts taken from other writers.
For other periods of history we have to take serious
account of Ephorus; but he can never be more to us
than an intermediary, and we must always bear in
mind that his mediation has at the same time produced
confusion.

Beside Ephorus let us put his kindred spirit Timaeus.
He certainly possessed a richer and more solid erudition;
even real research should by no means be totally denied
to him; on the other hand his unscrupulousness in working up his material was quite as great, and a plentiful
lack of taste must be added thereto. Thanks to its
subject, his work interested the Romans and remained
for a long time their model. This had important con-
sequences. There are traces of his influence in both
Cato and Varro; nay, even in Naevius.

One might have expected that a hero like Alexander,
an event like the conquest of the East, must have produced an historian. Alexander himself made all possible
provision for collecting the geographical material which
his expedition opened up. One can trace the effects of
the tradition of Hecataeus and Democritus which came
to him through Aristotle. He had also historians on his
staff—Anaximenes and Callisthenes; but no historical
result was achieved for the new countries, which can be
compared with the results of the Napoleonic expedition to
Egypt; and the king himself was as far from finding his
historian as he was from finding the Homer of whom he

dreamed. True, many of those who shared his marches
wrote down afterwards what had come under their own
observation, and an official and highly reliable account of
the campaigns saw the light. But a fantastic transformation of the hero and his deeds held the field from quite
early times, and maintained in tradition and literature a
life comparable to that changing existence which belongs
to Achilles and Odysseus from Homer onwards in tragedy,
in poetical and prose stories, down eventually to Dictys
and Dares. Alexander became the two-horned hero
of fable who still bears his name in the East ; and the
same mythical image of him permeates the Middle Ages.
But did the learned men of antiquity ever make so much
as a serious attempt to ascertain the truth ? We see
particularly well in Plutarch how the compilers of the
Alexandrian age did nothing but put together, with much
industry and no criticism, a mass of variant statements ;
and we rightly count it as a great achievement for his
time that Arrian selected out of the mass two books,
as old and, in his judgement, as trustworthy as could be
found, and worked them into one.

While Ephorus was compiling his universal history
of the Greeks—for his horizon extended no further—
Aristotle was setting members of his school to work at
his great collections—collections of constitutions, collections of legal codes, and others. His material was in part
the same, but the extent of his work infinitely wider.
In greatness of aim the undertaking was fully comparable
with his work in Natural Science. On many occasions
he researched among documents himself ; for instance,
we now know he did so in editing the genuine Delphic
Chronicle. The value of inscriptions and archives, of
popular songs and proverbs, was quite familiar to him ;
but for the most part he was already able to operate with

published material. That means that the same spirit
which he exhibited on a large scale was already spread
abroad, and had even in the fifth century guided others
besides Hellanicus, who composed quite a number of local
chronicles. Demetrius, the disciple of Aristotle, carried
his master's methods to Egypt, and the collection of the
Alexandrian Library assured for the next generation
the possibility of systematically excerpting the extant
historical literature, as was done, for instance, by Callimachus and his disciples. Yet the production of local
histories went on for a long time. In Athens, indeed,
the *Atthis*, or Athenian chronicle, disappeared with the
loss of political liberty in the Chremonidean War ; but
where liberty survived, as in Rhodes and Heraclea,
there was also a local literature right to the end of the
Hellenistic period. What later writings of the sort there
may have been, is a subject which has still been too
little studied to be taken account of here. In working
over the material, also, Alexandria stood by no means
alone ; a man like Polemon of Ilion actually worked at
inscriptions. What a wealth of material there was
becomes obvious as soon as we look at any of the rather
richer excerpts of Hellenistic literature, for example,
the excerpts in Strabo of the treatise on the 'Catalogue
of Ships' by Apollodorus of Athens. It is a pressing
duty of classical learning, besides the reconstruction of
the lost works of history, for which much is still to be
done, to collect this material which is associated with
definite localities, without reference to the authors'
names. Perhaps the project will be treated at the
International Historical Congress. If, however, we ask
the question whether the learned men of that time understood how to make any proper use of their treasures,
the answer must be unfortunately in the negative. Now

that we possess his *Constitution of Athens* we canno'
conceal from ourselves that Aristotle was no historian
and no other arose after him. No doubt Eratosthenes
was a *savant* of imposing powers, even in his chronology.
No doubt modern research has been at times too ready to
refuse consideration to the dates which a man like Apollodorus embodied in his metrical chronicle ; but in general,
what we call historical criticism was not only not attained,
but not so much as sought after. Here the new commen-
tary of Didymus on Demosthenes gives us an example,
which is all the more instructive that it depends upon
Hermippus the Callimachean. Hermîas of Atarneus, the
friend of Aristotle, was described by contemporary historians in the most contradictory terms. Hermippus simply
sets their accounts down side by side. He never so much
as thinks of wishing to reach the truth. The lives of the
classical poets—for instance that of Sophocles, which
owes much to Ister and shows the use of documents—
are equally rich and equally uncritical. It was grammarians almost exclusively who collected such excerpts,
and those who used the books so made were again chiefly
grammarians. When towards the end of the Hellenistic
period there arose a demand for Histories of the World,
which was satisfied by Agatharchides, Castor, Diodorus,
Nicolaus, we remark with surprise and disappointment
how little these historians know the material so conve-
niently prepared for them—far less know how to estimate
it. Imagine an even tolerably educated modern historian
put to work in the library of Alexandria : what a history
of ancient Greece he could put together, merely out of
the books ! But Diodorus made extracts from Ephorus,
nothing further ; and Nicolaus sought for romances
rather than documents. Let us take to heart the fact
that the Hellenistic scholars, the flower of Greek

learning, made no attempt at all at proceeding to scientific synthesis.

Contemporary history indeed was written even at that time by distinguished men, almost all of them practical politicians, like Thucydides. His spirit was never quite lost to remembrance, and his example constantly stimulated new followers till far on in the Byzantine Age. But let us take as an example the only man whose work is to a large extent preserved, Polybius. For the time which he is the first to describe, he works on the archives of Rome, Aegion, and Rhodes ; but how far does his research go for the older time, for which he is still our standard authority ? Not more than two books, narratives from the opposing camps, are used by him for the first Punic war ; and when-he has criticized them, by means merely of general considerations, he thinks he has done enough. In the same way he compares Aratus and Phylarchus. How poverty-stricken is his contribution to the earliest history of his own state, the Achaean League ! He himself was in antiquity as much the standard authority for the period from 222 to 146, as Thucydides was for the Peloponnesian War. We are the first who have troubled ourselves to complete him from documents, and to correct his often prejudiced judgements. Is it not obvious that no real historical research existed either in theory or practice ? The many words which Polybius devotes to his own method and to the criticism of Ephorus and Timaeus are at bottom as *banal* as Lucian's essay on the writing of history.

We are not entirely without knowledge of the ancient Greek theory of education. At latest in the school of Posidonius—and I think a little earlier—the so-called ἐγκύκλιος παιδεία, or 'universal instruction', was formed into a system which has continued to our own

Universities in the form of ' the seven liberal arts '. The
study of history has no place in it ; astronomy, archi-
tecture, and medicine have ! It follows that the Greeks
and Romans had no education in history. Here again,
the clearest evidence is given us by the grammatical
hand-book of Dionysius Thrax with its scholia, and next
to him perhaps by Quintilian. The Grammarian mentions
as part of his *métier*, if he proposes to expound the classics,
ἱστοριῶν πρόχειρος ἀπόδοσις. Stories to which the poet
alludes must be familiar to his commentator. That
led of course to instruction in the so-called mythical
history. In that department we have school compo-
sitions in the Papyri, and school compendia like the
Bibliotheca attributed to Apollodorus. Real history
also occurs in the better class of scholia, like those to
Aeschines ; but very rarely and only as occasion demands.
No word need be lost upon the sovereign freedom of
invention which was allowed to the rhetor with regard to
history, and equally with regard to law. But one final
piece of evidence. The sceptical philosophy—probably
in the time of Carneades, since it can scarcely be the
work of Ainesidemus and his school—undertook to
disprove the possibility of scientific knowledge in all
the special sciences. Grammar, rhetoric, dialectic, even
music and astrology are treated ; of history there is not
a word.

The facts are now before our eyes : let us inquire into
the causes.

It seems a contradiction that a nation which was the
first on the earth to produce an historian, the nation of
Herodotus and Thucydides, never attained to a science
of history ; but that is explained by the history of this
people, its heroic greatness and its tragic fate. In the
same century in which Buddha among the unhistoried

Indians founded religion upon a rejection of life; in which the Jews through the loss of their national state were reduced to founding a church as a substitute, and in demanding universal validity for their national god conceived of their national hopes as realized in the future ; the Ionians, also under the dominion of foreign races, emancipated themselves from State and from Church alike. What remained was the individual and the universe, and even the latter threatened to forfeit its objective reality, and to exist only in the imagination of the per-cipient subject. Yet at that time, through the obser-vation that eternal and ascertainable laws hold sway in the movement of the heavenly bodies, the Ionians arrived at the revelation that all life is a unity, and is permeated not by chance or caprice, but by law and reason, *logos*. As a postulate of intellect—we had better perhaps say, of belief—they recognized that these laws must be knowable by the human reason, and they did their best to know them. That led to natural science, and opened the way through mathematics to logic. But there was no way leading from there to history, neither from Heraclitus nor from Parmenides nor yet from Pythagoras.

Then the Athenians created the free state, which seemed to them to be the rational ideal, the State in itself, and at the same time was intended to afford scope to the free individual. While this state held up its head, while they lived history and made history, the ground was prepared for men who wrote history. The Athenian democracy, like the emancipation from all authority which came from Ionia, is a first condition for the appearance of Herodotus and Thucydides ; and no doubt the incomparably rich intellectual life which Socrates saw around him, contained in itself the seeds of historical science, as of so much else

which was not to see the light until modern times. But
the Athenian empire collapsed ; the democracy showed
itself incapable of founding the national state ; and on
the ruins there arose that phantom growth of rhetoric
and sophistic which renounced the search after truth
and honesty, and which brought to shipwreck first the
learning and then the whole civilization of antiquity.
Individualism and egoism raised their heads again :
Cynics, Cyrenaics, Democriteans ignore society if they
do not hate it.   Plato, indeed, creates for knowledge a
place which the storms of political life cannot destroy,
but the basis of his instruction lies in mathematical
and physical science.   True, he does not neglect duties
to society, but he seeks the new foundation, which
they certainly needed, elsewhere than on the ground
of history.   No doubt he had thought on this subject,
as on others, more profoundly than most people recognize.   Any one who has read his *Laws* aright cannot
deny that the conception of historical development was
familiar to him ; but his mind is devoted to eternal
Being ; how can the realm of Becoming, how can that
which is past, be to him the object of true knowledge ?
If we look at the enormous endeavours which Aristotle
made for the amassing of historical material, we are
inclined to think that the ascertaining of historical truth
was an end to him.   And yet it is not so.   Wonderful
as was his power of describing the historical development
of thought, as shown in the introductions of his philosophical lectures, now that we read his *Constitution of
Athens* we know that he was no historian.   His great
collections afforded material for his political and ethical
theories.   On these subjects and on rhetoric he gave
public lectures.   No man in antiquity ever gave lectures
on history.

But there is another element in the case which reaches
even deeper into the nature of the Hellenic genius. The
history of the past can be understood by no man who
cannot transport himself into the souls of men passed
away. That idea never came near to the Greeks ; they
never tried to think on the model of foreign peoples.
In general they show themselves little sensitive to the
individuality of others. The psychology of the Socratic
school, and above all that of the Stoa and of Epicurus,
begins and ends with the normal man. Woman and child
are to them merely imperfect man. Even the keen
observation of Theophrastus discovers no characteristics
of individuals ; only of types. What enormous advan-
tages that conferred upon their philosophy and their
plastic art I need not say ; but the light was not without
its shadow. Their biographical writings began with
ideal figures—with Heracles and Pythagoras, and they
never even attempted to show the development of a human
soul. How we moderns admire those of their poets who
succeed in the delineation of individual men ! How we
exult that we have a glimpse of it again in Menander !
But how rare such poets are, and how keenly one must
look in order to seize the individual quality in their
creations ! Here also no one has done higher service
than Plato, and yet his most ardent admirer will not deny
that by the laws of his whole being he was bound
to take an alien, nay, a hostile attitude towards real
historical research — as, for instance, he never read
Thucydides.

I have difficulty in resisting the temptation to draw
conclusions for our own guidance in pursuing historical
research. Is it not obvious that nothing at all depends
on the compilers ? What they add is nothing but a confusion of the original tradition. They must therefore be

set aside and the true tradition reinstated, fragmentary as it may be. And though we do not often succeed in naming the original author of a statement, still, thanks especially to epigraphic discovery and research, we can to a certain extent from the content of a given statement estimate its origin and value. Very often, no doubt, we can only establish the conclusion that it refers to times and conditions of which the ancients cannot have had any trustworthy information and consequently fell back upon hypotheses which bind no one. But at least it is well to be conscious of what we do not and cannot know. And yet far too great a part of all the most modern statements about the ethnography and history, law and religion, of the oldest times rests upon ancient hypotheses and inventions, arbitrarily selected and never put to proof. But I must hasten on, in mere justice, to treat the Greek historians from another side.

Even of Herodotus it holds good, that in the wonderful story of Croesus all that charms us is the work of fiction— the death of Atys, the conversation with Solon, the deliverance of Croesus from death. Let us look next at Ctesias. Not only Semiramis and Sardanapallus, but even what he tells of the Persian kings at whose courts he had lived, is for the most part fiction, though fiction of an effective kind and by no means lacking in the true oriental colour. Xenophon learned in the school of Ctesias ; and, though he only partially reached it, he set before himself in the Cyropaedeia no lesser goal than Ctesias. If Clitarchus describes how the queen of the Amazons sweeps down from the far north to offer the conqueror of the world her love, that is fiction, but magnificent fiction. In other words, Greek historical writing, from the Ionians onward, had a much wider range

than that to which Thucydides the Athenian statesman
wished to confine it. It embraced what we call romance
and the Novel. It is just in this that History shows
herself the successor of the Epos. I have no doubt that
she was also affected by a very strong influence from the
literatures of the East, for there we find exactly the same
' Novels ', and there also they are hung upon the historical tradition, or at least upon famous historical
persons. Even in the stories of the Egyptians that is the
case ; and it remains so in the *Thousand and One Nights*.
We have now in Berlin remains of the romance of Achikar
written in the fifth century before Christ, in Aramaic,
which point directly to Nineveh. Democritus is said to
have introduced this romance into Greece, where later
on it was transferred to Aesop. While the Ionians, in
the sixth century, already weary of the Heroic Epos,
were turning themselves to the historic novel, the Epic
Saga in Athens underwent a renewal and intensification
in tragedy. Tragedy, without giving up its exalted
style, proceeded steadily on the road of assimilating its
characters and its plots to real life. And after a hundred
years people were tired even in Athens of always looking
at the heroes. It is quite intelligible but still very noteworthy, that the art of historical narrative deliberately
sought to compete with tragedy. True, Aristotle wrote
the *Poetics* for poets, and unkindly relegated history to
a subordinate position. But members of his school
attempted successfully to turn the tragic arts to account
in *Historiê*. In fact, a man who had lived through the
times of Cassander, Demetrius, Agathocles, showed no
bad taste if he counted these figures to the full as tragic
as Orestes and Medea. And no less laudable was it in
him to compose no historical tragedies, but to write
history. That is what Duris of Samos did. We must

admit that no history in the style of Thucydides or
Hieronymus was produced thereby; it was history in the
style of Sir Walter Scott. But are we not pedants if we
take that amiss in Duris ? Myron of Priene invented the
story of Aristodemus at Ithome, as Scott invented the
moving history of Ivanhoe. We are pedants if we treat
as history the story of the first Messenian war ; and it is
just the same with Tarquinius Superbus and Lucretia,
with Coriolanus and Verginia. But these stories do not
cease to be beautiful because they are fiction. It is only
necessary to put each element in its proper place, and
to recognize that historical romance played no small
part in Greek literature.

Meanwhile we must never forget that we make a dis-
tinction which the ancients do not know. Their fully
developed theory of prose, or more accurately of *Eloquentia*, as we find it in Cicero and Dionysius, though
peripatetic in its origin, has been developed from beginning
to end in the spirit of rhetoric. Consequently it knows
only of formal divisions ; so that even poetry is only
a species of *Eloquentia* conditioned by verse and style.
Accordingly, Epos and *Historié* may have the same
material, as, for instance, Lucan and Silius have simply
taken Livy for their basis. It need not, therefore, surprise us that the Love-story, which we place quite far
from history and near to poetry, among the Greeks
belonged definitely to the former, even though the same
material may have been treated in Epic'or Elegiac form.
We find it in Ctesias, certainly under the influence of
the East ; we find it in Xenophon ; and now that we
possess the remnants of the Ninos-romance the bridge is
thrown across to the so-called Erotici. The oldest book
of the sort which is completely preserved, by Chariton
of Aphrodisias, shows the connexion still quite clearly ;

for the romance is not only definitely dated at the end
of the fifth century, but the Persian dominion in Asia
Minor provides something more than the historical back-
ground.   The Love-story itself has of course another
origin ; it springs from the New Comedy.   And is it not
easy to understand how a period which saw no more tragic
events, the period of peace inaugurated by the Empire,
was attracted by plots taken from the every-day life of
citizens ?   It was just the same cause which brought the
citizens of Menander upon the stage in place of the
heroes of Euripides.   This New Comedy element grew
steadily stronger, and with the decay of culture the
historical nucleus became more and more shadowy.   But
it was not abandoned easily.   The first Christian romance,
which borrows from comedy the motive of the discovery
of lost children, makes them spring from the family of
Trajan ; and the history of Apollonius of Tyre, which
Shakespeare thought worthy of dramatic treatment,
starts from king Antiochus, to whom it transfers an old
tragic legendary motive.   Thus even these insignificant
productions can teach us a surprising amount as to the
continued life and transformation of the historical
memories and the poetical types of the people.   But
one thing we must confess need never be looked for,
the very quality in which lies the strength of modern
historical romance.   An industry such as Flaubert spent,
I might almost say squandered, upon *Salammbô*, is even
at the present time an exception, but at least the principle
will be admitted by all, that the choice of an historical
subject demands the greatest possible truth and colour,
both local and historical.   That is a point of which the
ancient romance-writers never thought.   Who could
demand it, when even the most serious historians are
scarcely more conscientious ?

Let us raise ourselves for a moment out of these low levels to the proper heights of historiography. Even Tacitus took over material already formed, and worked it up as seemed to him good, not only in the *Annals*, but also in the surviving parts of the *Histories*. Many people here fight against the evidence, merely because they do not sufficiently see with what means and what methods the historian of that time used to work. No man to-day can make any pretensions to be treated seriously, if he thinks of Tiberius, as a ruler or as a man, as Tacitus has described him. Tacitus received from his predecessors the false outlines ; he held to them without testing them ; and then he threw in from his own art that psychological painting whose completeness no Greek ever attained. That makes the picture only so much the further from truth. Ought we therefore to reproach Tacitus with a lack of honesty ? Let us compare him with Posidonius. Posidonius knew what Science was— a thing no Roman ever dreamed of. Yet how does he describe to us the history and the characters of the Gracchi ? Even in our jejune extracts one cannot help seeing in Gaius, sinking deeper and deeper under the passions of political strife till he falls into outbreaks of tyrannical madness, a character that would pass even in Shakespeare's histories. But how little care for accuracy there was, even in the main events, is shown by the fact that Posidonius represents Nasica as the murderer of Tiberius. How was it possible for a man like Posidonius to go so utterly wrong ? I venture to hope that the answer has been given. What we call 'research' was in the region of history a thing unknown to him. He left to the grammarian the labour of inquiry into detail, as by the side of Tacitus there stands Suetonius, whom the senator and orator regards as far below him. It

may be that Mr. Dryasdust is no very agreeable com-
panion, but he is indispensable. It is the curse of ancient
historical writing that it neglected him. Very famous
persons have tried to do the same in our own days.
The result is the same, but they have the less claim
upon our forgiveness. If, however, Posidonius and
Tacitus made free play with the material which they
had, and with which they simply rested content—if they
then proceeded, of their own strength, to produce complete pictures of events and men, they did so as poets,
as artists ; and what they did was within their rights.
Gibbon, too, acted in the same way, and therein lies
his greatness. Yet let us be honest. We ourselves, when
once Dryasdust has done his work within us, and we
advance to the shaping of our scientific results—from
that time forth we do just the same, we use our free
formative imagination. The tradition yields us only
ruins. The more closely we test and examine them,
the more clearly we see how ruinous they are ; and out
of ruins no whole can be built.   The tradition is dead ;
our task is to revivify life that has passed away. We
know that ghosts cannot speak until they have drunk
blood ; and the spirits which we evoke demand the
blood of our hearts. We give it to them gladly ; but
if they then abide our question, something from us has
entered into them ; something alien, that must be cast
out, cast out in the name of truth ! For Truth is a stern
goddess ; she knows no respect of persons, and her handmaid, Science, strides ever onward, beyond Posidonius
and Tacitus, beyond Gibbon and Mommsen, even though,
so far as art has ennobled them, these men's works may
endure. Because we have over the Greeks the advantage
of possessing a science of history, the greatest of us can
no longer claim the sort of authority which belonged for

centuries even to a man like Livy. But he who is worthy to serve the immortal goddess resigns himself gladly to the transitory life of his works. And he has also the comfort that in Science there is no defeat, if only his torch is handed on still burning to his successor.

τοιοίδε τοί μοι λαμπαδηφόρων δρόμοι,
νικᾶι δ᾽ ὁ πρῶτος καὶ τελευταῖος δραμών.

APOLLO

How the great public in England conceives of Apollo, I will not venture to surmise. On the Continent he remains for such circles practically the same as Raphael painted him in his Parnassos, the heavenly fiddler. The town in which I live has set up a monument to our Emperor Frederick. It was desired to suggest that he had taken an interest in Art and Science, and with that object two pillars have been set up behind him surmounted by Athena and Apollo, the latter—as was to be expected— reminding us in figure and drapery of the Apollo Belvedere, which has been since Winckelmann the most popular work of Greek sculpture. The god of the poets and the *cafés chantants* is of course derived from Roman poetry and its modern imitations, now obsolete. It was a step in advance when Sculpture led us to the conception that Apollo embodied the fullness of manly beauty and the strength of youth. But for many years that advance bred confusion in Archaeology, since all the youthful standing figures of archaic art were incontinently put down as Apollos, even though the circumstances of their discovery proved them to be funeral statues, as, for instance, the Apollo of Tenea. Even those discovered in sanctuaries of Apollo are simply statues of men, and represent men dedicated to the God, just as the very common figures of beasts in bronze or clay represent sacrificial animals. On the Colossus of Naxos there is inscribed the actual word ἀνδριάς, ' figure of a man ' ; and yet it has been misinterpreted. People forgot that for genuine religious feeling mere beauty cannot suffice to characterize a god. Simple presentation in human shape, however beautiful or however ugly, says nothing. In the archaic period a god can only be characterized by his attributes.

If we carry our question to those who profess some higher culture, the commonest answer we shall receive will be that Apollo is the Sun. Even among mythologists that idea is widespread, and Otfried Müller roused strong opposition when he denied it. Nay, when he brought on his death by working too hard under the August sun at Delphi, the epigram gained currency that Apollo had slain him for denying his solar nature. In the first line this interpretation, like the other, is derived from Roman poetry. We may be sure, for instance, that Vergil would have seriously maintained it. But no doubt it is really far older ; but unfortunately it is a theological explanation ; and, though a theological explanation may always indicate something of importance for the real religious idea, it is never authoritative and only too often misleading. For theology does not arise until men find it necessary to justify their religious feelings at the bar of their reason. We will follow our own historical method, and address our question to the Greeks themselves, who believed in Apollo not because he was a personification, but because he was a person and a God. We begin naturally with Homer.

There we see at once the importance of what Apollo does not do. He makes no music ; no prophecy ; no love to the daughters of men ; all of which things he does so freely in Hesiod and Pindar. He wears his hair unshorn ; in other respects we receive, as usual, little precise information about the god's bodily presence. A mighty god he is, and of mighty deeds ; greatest of the sons of Zeus. The bow is his terrible weapon. He helps none but the Trojans, and he has a house on their

citadel. He beats back Diomedes ; he causes the death
of Patroclus, and Achilles knows that he will cause his
own. He addresses him as ' Most deadly of the gods.'
In the very first book of the *Iliad* the god enters in his
majesty. As he strides down from Olympus to send his
arrows of pestilence upon the Achaean host, because his
priest has been wronged, the poet says that ' he walked
like unto the night ', ὃ δ' ἤιε νυκτὶ Ϝεϝοικώς. Our northern
lands do not understand the phrase. But any one
who has felt the descent of Night on the Aegean sea,
sudden, irresistible, unearthly, may form some idea how
the terrible god came down to execute judgement. The
being who was like this Night can scarcely have been
a sun-god.

Homer mentions quite a number of places sacred to
the god in Asia. He mentions Delos with special honour.
The only reference to Delphi and its treasures comes in
a poem whose geographical horizon is different from all
the rest. We can of our own knowledge greatly increase
the number of these sanctuaries on the Asiatic coasts ;
and their pre-hellenic names prove that they reach back
far beyond the time of Homer : Klaros, Caucasa, Didyma
—for this last is formed like Sidyma, and has nothing to
do with twins. Lycia especially always treated Apollo
as its ancestral god. His holy places there are numerous ;
he was born in Araxa. Delos, his Greek birthplace,
belongs geographically and ethnographically to the same
area. In Delos the topography tells a plain tale : what
I am saying now was taught me by an expedition to
Kynthos. The palm-tree which was a marvel to Odysseus
stood down below on the holy lake ; and the sanctuaries
of Hellenic times were congregated round the same spot.
But there is a far more impressive shrine in the cave on
the summit of Kynthos, which was wrought into a sanc-

tuary in pre-hellenic times, with a prodigal expenditure of labour but also with great skill. It, one would fain believe, was the dwelling of the Lord of that island round which the Cyclades danced. Didyma, too, has a view far over land and sea ; Klaros on the contrary lies in seclusion. There was a cave there, however, just as on Kynthos ; and the Sibyl, Apollo's handmaid, lived everywhere in a cave.

As to the nature of this Delian god, the hymn of the blind bard of Chios gives us a distinct picture, which reaches at least as far back as the seventh century, and is still in agreement with the *Iliad*. I quote a piece of the introduction, which describes the epiphany of the God in Olympus. Editors have not understood the composition of the hymn, and in consequence have often rejected these verses, which nevertheless bear the mark of high antiquity.

He moved, and lo, on Olympus the high gods shook with
    dread ;
Nearer he came and nearer, and up in amaze they fled
Away from their seats in heaven, as he bent the bow of
    his pride ;
Leto alone stood fast by Zeus the Thunderer's side.
And she loosened the mighty bow-string and folded the
    quiver-lid,
And with both hands from his shoulders the fearful bow
    undid,
And hung it high on a pillar which the Father named
    his own
On a golden nail ; and led him and throned him on his
    throne.
And the Father poured him nectar, and lifted the carven
    gold
And pledged the Son of his love. Then back on their
    seats of old
The gods in peace did seat them, and Leto's heart was high
To have borne a wondrous Bowman and a Lord of
    valiancy.

Apollo, then, is the son of Zeus and beloved by his
father ; but the gods of the Greeks stand in fear of him.
How much more must the Greeks themselves fear him ?
Those of the *Iliad* have good reason, for he helps their
enemies. And, as we have seen, the seats of his worship
are pre-hellenic. This gives us one of two conclusions.
Either the Greek colonists adopted this god together
with his sacred sites—in that case he is an Asiatic ; or
else they brought a god with them whom they identified
with the pre-hellenic god. This is quite conceivable,
for it is what actually happened with the Greek Artemis,
who in more places than Ephesus was assimilated
to an Asiatic Nature-goddess, who had little essential
likeness to her and really became Greek only in name.
If Apollo was not originally Greek, then it was in Asia
that Artemis first acquired a brother and mother ; and
they were as a matter of fact quite unessential to her
cultus. To decide the question we must naturally go to
Greece proper ; but I wish first to remain on the ground
which we now tread. In this region, the point is decided
by the mother, Leto. She does not exist at all in Greece
proper except as coming in the train of Apollo. I ad-
vanced this thesis which I am now expounding some
years ago in a short article (*Hermes* 38). And it came
as a welcome confirmation of my views to find Leto
definitely bearing the epithet ' Asiatic ' in an unpub-
lished inscription from Argos. Nowhere but in Lycia
has she a real cultus ; nowhere but in Lycia are men
named after her. And one of the few Lycian words
whose meaning is certain is *Lada*, ' woman.' That Lato
is the name of a place in Crete agrees with this very
well, for the Lycians are intimately connected with Crete.
Lastly, in very early times, though not in Homer, Apollo
bears the name ' Letoïdes ' ; it is the only metronymic in

Olympus, and it was only among the Lycians that sons bore their mothers' names. If we ever succeed in making out the Lycian language, perhaps the name Apollo, which has hitherto defied serious explanation, may at last be interpreted.

Of the cultus of this god there is not much to be said. Even the innumerable inscriptions from Delos are rather barren of results. It was a surprise to scholars to find that a sacred cave was so usual. It follows that, in the period from which our information comes, the cave had ceased to matter. Without doubt the god must at one time have practised prophecy everywhere ; but none of the Asiatic oracles had any great importance in the period known to us. Heraclitus, writing in Ephesus, speaks of the ' lord of Delphi ' as the prophet. There must in very early times have been human prophets connected with the god. Even Kalchas is in reality the representative of Klaros. The transition from prophecy to poetry and music is an easy one ; yet the old poets invoke the Muses, not Apollo ; and it is not till we come to Hesiod and Greece proper that the Muses form a choir for Apollo's harping. In the Homer-legend, too, Apollo plays no part. On the other hand, it can be made out with certainty that his worship demanded processions and dancing, to which singing was gradually added. The meaning of the word *Molpé* passes gradually from 'dance' to ' song ', and colleges of Molpoi are now known to us in many parts of Ionia, especially in Miletus. In Delos the maidens dance to Apollo at all periods of history. The Paean, the Procession, and the Song are characteristic of his cultus in Delos, and have spread from thence in every direction. The communities which meet for his worship send him choirs of youths and maidens. In Athens also, the oldest extant inscription is about a dancer

of Apollo. His festivals are by no means as firmly fixed
in the natural year as those of Dionysus, and within the
month his holy day is sometimes the new moon, sometimes the first quarter, sometimes the twentieth. His
essential character cannot possibly be derived from the
life of Nature. For if, for example, in the barren island
of Delos, the festivals partly relate to agriculture, and
the Thargelia, or feast of first-fruits, is sacred to Apollo
among all the Ionians, not much can be deduced from
that. The god to whom the land belongs cannot possibly
be neglected on such occasions, whatever his original
nature may have been. Of course also, when the Greeks
took over the local god, there was much transference of
attributes. Only one thing is obviously peculiar to
Apollo from the outset. He is not permanently present
in his temple, but comes there, invited and welcomed by
his special communities or the choir of dancers which
represents them. The god's epiphany in heaven, which
the poet described to us, has its analogy in the epiphany
on earth. Callimachus has a brilliant description of one.
This conception seems scarcely Hellenic. It holds good of
Dionysus also ; but Dionysus is equally a foreign god.

We can thus reach a sort of conception of this eastern
Apollo, as he held sway in the lives and hearts of the
Ionians from the time of Homer on ; but it were vain to
try to point out the ultimate roots of his being and say
how he first became a god. We cannot expect it other-
wise, for it was not the Greeks who made him a god. He
was already a person when they came, a person of more
or less definite appearance and character, the Lord of
the land and of the greatest sanctuaries. They learned
the rites of his cult from his old worshippers. First, he
was mostly the alien and hostile god, who must needs
be appeased. Gradually he undertook the work of

protection. The sender of evil also averted it, and taught
how it could be exorcized. Then more and more Hellenic
elements were added to him. But his essential nature
was already fixed, and it remained unshaken.

When the birth of Apollo in Delos became an accepted
fact, it followed as a matter of course that he must at
some time have set forth from there and taken possession
of his other sanctuaries, not merely of the 'Delia' which
actually existed in many places, but of all. Naturally
this belief proves nothing ; but in the West we shall find
it suit the facts. It will hardly be doubted in the case
of Euboea and Attica, because these countries are really
closely connected with Delos. But Boeotia too had a
Delion, and it forms the starting-point of a sacred road
to Delphi. On this theory it follows that the sanctuaries
of Apollo, at any rate under that name, must be comparatively late. And, as a matter of fact, this is often
obvious : for instance, at Thebes, where the sanctuary
lies far outside the city. A noteworthy conclusion can
be drawn from the discoveries made by the French at
the Ptoion, discoveries full of important results but
unfortunately not yet satisfactorily published. There,
in a hidden wooded dell, high on the mountain-chain,
stood that Temple which enjoyed such high repute in
the days of Pindar. The oldest sanctuary seems to have
been a little cave beautifully walled in the polygonal
style. But this in itself is not primaeval ; and corre-
spondingly, nothing has been found which reaches to
the so-called Mycenaean time. It follows that the god
did not appear there till comparatively late, presumably from Delos, as Pindar describes. And then
Delphi. No doubt evidences have been found to show
the primaeval sanctity of the region ; and the face of
Nature impresses even now upon every traveller the

conviction that it is a holy spot. The pre-hellenic names
Parnassos and Castalia speak clear. But the pre-hellenic
element is forgotten. The old possessors of the region,
who never lost their worship, are the true Greek gods
Gaia and Poseidon, Earth and the Husband of Earth ;
both names are transparent. And similarly both in
tradition and cultus it is never forgotten that Apollo
made himself master of Delphi by conquest. The representative of the holy Mother, Earth, is merely transformed
into the horrible dragon that Apollo had to overpower.
It is clear, therefore, in the first place, that the cultus
was imported, and imported from the East ; for all the
roads of the processions to Delphi come from that quarter.
In the second place, it is clear that the battle with the
dragon means nothing more than the expulsion of an
old god by a new, and consequently tells us nothing
about the true nature of Apollo. The festival com-
memorating this battle and the whole story of the dragon
are local through and through.

When Apollo had conquered Delphi, it became the
centre for the spread of his worship in many directions.
In all places where he is worshipped as Pythios, it is
not his general Apolline nature, but the specifically
Delphic element, that forms the decisive factor. He is
Pythios in Athens ; it was only as Pythios and in quite
late times that he became the ancestor of the Athenians.
He is Pythian (πυθαεύς) also in Epidaurus and Argos.
It was as Pythios that he gave help to Lycurgus of
Sparta. There even the Apollo of Amyclae is an invader
who has expelled the pre-hellenic god Hyakinthos. In
Crete the god is Pythios everywhere ; the primaeval
temple of Gortyn is a Pythion. The Thessalian cult
cannot be separated from Delphi. It need not be dis-
puted that in many places there must have been an

C 2

older Apollo-cult, which only gradually reconciled itself to the Pythian. That gives us all we are arguing for. The process reaches far into the East. Even at Miletus Apollo Delphinios was set up by the side of Apollo of Didyma; and Artemis at any rate had the epithet Pythian, which is the more striking as at Pytho she has scarcely any significance.

Apollo Delphinios is the god who in the shape of his sacred dolphin showed the way to the colonists who crossed the seas in his service. On land he did the same in the form of a raven. Such legends are the marks left by the spread of Apollo worship and, in later times, by the migrations of the Greeks who felt themselves to be his servants. The dolphin and the Delphians bear kindred names; true, we must not imagine that Delphinios was always the Pythios of Delphi; but Pythios may well have succeeded in claiming for his own the shrines of Delphinios.

It is of this Delphian god that we have now to speak. It is no matter now what he once was, before he took possession of Delphi; no matter what rites were practised in the places affiliated to Delphi. Nay, even the ceremonial and cultus of the Delphians has no real significance. On the other hand, there has now arisen something which deserves the name of religion in a higher sense, a community of faith which even passes beyond the boundaries of the nation; a faith which often determines the action both of individuals and of states; and which, though, like every real religion, morality is neither its cause nor its aim, ends nevertheless by exerting a conscious moral influence.

The date of this transformation, the importance of which cannot be over-emphasized, may be to some extent made out. It is fixed on the one side by the fact that

Hesiod is still uninfluenced by the specific god of Delphi ;
on the other, by the war waged by the Amphictyons
soon after 600 B. C. in order to make the priests of the
god independent and to provide the Temple with a
harbour and free access to the sea. Such co-operation
among different tribes can only have been produced by
a very firm belief in the god. In material things it is
only after this war that Delphi advances to the height
of her power. In the time of Pisistratus the temple was
burnt down, and the whole world far beyond the boundaries of Hellenism contributed the means of adorning
that sanctuary which the French excavations have enabled
us to tread once more. The power of Delphi was still
undiminished. But by that time political and other earthly
considerations must have begun to play their part. The
spiritual strength of the oracle had been at its highest
earlier, when it awakened in men's hearts the belief that
a God sat abidingly at Delphi, who was able and
ready in his all-wisdom to afford them help and counsel
in the hardest situations of life.

Of the *Prophêtai* who gave this decisive turn to the
religion of Apollo every trace is lost. And I will not
indulge in surmises. But the result can easily be made
out from the periods of which we have adequate knowledge. Even Herodotus is evidence enough. It is only
in Delphi that the god deals out the revelations of truth.
He no longer visits the affiliated sanctuaries, or at least
he does not hold converse with the faithful in them.
How he breathes his spirit into the priestess remains
a sacred mystery. The rationalist fables about a cleft
in the earth and intoxicating vapours deserve no word
of refutation. The priests are fain to give the revelation
shape in the only form of literature then existing, Homeric
verse. That in itself proves that the god intends to

exercise an international influence. It proves at the same
time the existence of Delphic poetry, which must surely
be responsible for the fact that in the current form of
the Heroic Saga the action is usually set going by means
of Delphic oracles, and a spirit of propaganda on behalf of
the Delphic religion is often quite visible. We can understand now why the laurel, which the god loves for its puri-
fying properties, has come to form the crown of the poet.

In Delphi, then, there is a place where every man,
after the performance of a definite ritual, can obtain an
answer to all questions; and the god who answers is
recognized as possessing all knowledge and all wisdom.
The advice which private persons obtain in their private
difficulties is a secondary matter. Oracles of that sort
were often given, sometimes even in writing. We know
this best of remote places like Dodona, where the belief
in such oracles continued even in Hellenistic times. The
special note of Delphi is that men turn to the god in
difficulties of conscience, and notably that States apply
to him to be delivered from war and sedition, from
famine and pestilence. They act on the assumption
that the cause of the evil is some sin against the god
of which they are unconscious, or else some angry ghost,
whom only Apollo knows and can avert. He does so
by means of a rite of atonement with a cleansing which
is corporeal through and through. We moderns have an
exact analogy in the realm of medicine. First all the
mischief must be ruthlessly removed; then there follows
a general disinfection. It begins commonly with a purification of the streets, presumably with sulphur. Besides
that come ritual observances, praying processions, sacri-
fices, foundings of shrines or buildings. There is no
mention, in the first instance, of any definitely moral
guilt; and for States moral guilt can only have a meta-

phorical meaning. But how could a world which attributed all misfortune to an offence against gods or spirits,
help ultimately addressing to the all-wise god of holiness
and purification the prayer : ' Lord, teach us how we
may live in purity ' ? And inasmuch as the god did
answer that prayer, he not only exerted a powerful
influence on law and morals, but actually introduced
into religion a new ethical element. We all know that
he made the avenging of blood an imperative duty upon
men ; Orestes slew his own mother at the god's command.
Yet the god also helped the State to reduce the avenging
of blood to a necessary part of its criminal law, as such
law gradually arose. We all know also how the constitution of state and society in Sparta on the one hand,
and the Athenian democracy on the other, came about
with the co-operation and under the guarantee of Delphi.
That shows us how the god desired to stand above parties,
just as he impartially accepted a tithe of the spoils in
every case of war. Even when he expressly took sides,
as in the Peloponnesian War, the Athenians against whom
he worked were not thereby prevented from seeking his
counsel in spiritual things. As a general rule, however,
it is the case that his political influence is exerted in the
direction which Sparta followed as its guiding principle.
He wished men in the state and society, as in religious
ritual, to remain true to the practice of their fathers.
He represented the conservative principle. One might
imagine that a god who claimed universal validity, and
thereby had raised himself above all others, might have
said, ' I am Apollo thy God, thou shalt have none other
gods but me.' But Apollo was no revolutionary. He
adhered to that first commandment which was impressed
upon all Greek children, ' Thou shalt honour the gods '—
that is, ' The gods of thy family and of thy city.' His

political attitude corresponded with this. Since at the
time when his religion shaped itself the Greek world was
based entirely on the family, and the state maintained
the fiction that it rested upon a community of blood,
the god himself was always the champion of this form
of society, if necessary by a fiction, as when he himself
became the ancestor of the Athenians. The state of
mind which he demanded can here also be traced back
to the second commandment laid upon every Greek child,
' Thou shalt honour thy father and thy mother,' with
its not infrequent corollary, ' Thou shalt love thy country.'
In the same way we can harmonize the Apolline morality
with the third commandment, ' Thou shalt obey the laws
which are common to all Greeks '—such as the duty of
respecting holy places and persons, of burying the dead
and revering the sanctity of the grave, of not rejecting
a suppliant for purification, of giving quarter in war.
And since the taking of oaths was of constant occurrence
both in legal matters and in ordinary social life, offences
in these departments fell naturally under the head of
'Ασέβεια (Impiety), or offence against a god. But this
applied morality, which may always be taken for granted,
is not the essential thing. It is the state of mind which
of itself takes form in such action that is really significant.
For this, all is summed up in the greeting which the god
addressed to each visitor of his temple—' Know thyself.'
By which was meant, ' Know that you are a mortal man,
weak and transitory, and know it here, face to face with
my eternal and divine majesty.' The consciousness that
man in complete isolation is completely helpless, and that
without the grace of the godhead he must sink in misery,
should bring him to walk in accordance with this spirit
and do everything to avoid the god's wrath. He has no
claim on the grace of God. He must bear contentedly

whatever the omnipotent ones choose to lay upon him.
¹ Man, what is he ? What is he not ? The dream of a
shadow; but when the god-given glory falls, then radiance
¹s laid upon a man and Life is gentle.' So at the
end of his life said Pindar, the most devout interpreter
of Apolline religion. All the deep sayings and parables,
which reiterate 'Observe the mean,' 'Be resigned,'
¹ Bethink thee of the end,' everything implied in that
specially Greek way of thinking which is summed up by
the untranslatable word σωφροσύνη, belongs to the γνῶθι
σαυτόν of the God. 'Live as though you must die to-
morrow, and yet as though you had fifty years before
you '; such was Apollo's precept to his friend Admetus.
For guerdon to the young builders of his temple the
god granted swift and happy death. The most gorgeous
offerings were accepted by him : but the scanty gift of
a pious peasant who lived in quietness remote and unknown to the world was pronounced by him to be what
he loved best. He laid down the most minute pre-
scriptions for external purification, but the words written
in the sanctuary of his son at Epidaurus were in his true
spirit : 'Pure must he be who enters the fragrant sanctuary; but purity is to have holy thoughts.'

It was after all only one side of Greek religious feeling
that the god revealed and demanded. To many it seems
to cover all that is characteristically Hellenic. They
fail to note that it is as alien to Homer as it is to the
great Athenians, with the single exception of Sophocles.
Since the rise of Delphi coincided with the supremacy
of the Dorians, Otfried Müller, with some show of justice,
held that this Apollo was a Dorian. But there is not
the spirit of any particular race in Apollo, and there is
a great deal more. We have reached a religion that
may address itself to humanity. It is a religion which

will always strongly attract the man who lets himself be guided by reason. It lays no account with another life, It practises, strictly speaking, no supernaturalism. It will adjust itself easily to natural authorities in the family and in society. It demands, however, in all momentous questions of life and religion some tribunal from which there is no appeal, such as Delphi was. Also, we must not forget what it lacks. It renounces the whole domain of mysticism; for its god has no direct communion with humanity. It renounces that disburdening of the soul which takes place in all forms of ecstasy, when man passes beyond himself. And therewith to a great extent it also renounces Hope, which in the lovely Hesiodic story was still left to mortal man. And lastly, there is no place in it for Progress, no place for that striving after the infinite by which Faust found for himself salvation. The self-knowledge of Apollo does not lead to individual self-dependence. A Socrates had to come and take up the mandate of the god, insisting, however, that man should know himself to be not only commanded but also enabled to do the good for the sake of the good.

By the time of Socrates and Plato many things had occurred to supersede in men's hearts the religion of Delphi. The medizing of the oracle was the smallest of them. For the Greeks bore Delphi no grudge on that count. But the national victory brought to light forces which would no longer submit to any external authority. The spirit of the Iono-Attic enlightenment and philosophy stood on its own feet and was irresistible. Aeschylus remained almost untouched by it, but his profound piety could not contentedly believe that the god had commanded matricide. It is in general noteworthy that Apollo never in any particular accords Woman her rights ; and it is the same with Pindar. For that reason alone

the Athenians must needs advance beyond him. In the
Eumenides of Aeschylus there is no justification of Apollo,
and the figure of Cassandra is a flaming protest against
his holiness. Euripides can actually say that the coun-
sellor of Orestes was a devil. Tragedy and comedy both
belong to Dionysus. That name brings before us a
religion which in its elements of mysticism and ecstasy
had always been an antithesis to that of Apollo. The
doctrine of a future life and retribution after death had
taken shape among the Orphic communities as early as
the sixth century B.C. In a word, the religion of Apollo
had done great service, but its mission was fulfilled.
New gods and greater had appeared, the greatest those
whose only temple was man's heart, and their only ritual
his life and thought.

The Delphic Apollo went on for many centuries giving
his oracles, celebrating his festivals, and maintaining his
external dignity, even though the munificence of his worshippers declined so greatly that to-day in his sanctuary
anything that comes from Hellenistic times strikes us as
alien and incongruous. Whatever may have been his origin
and character in this or that place, the Apollo worshipped
in common by all Greeks was by now a divinity of fairly
uniform content, a content to which Homer and Hesiod,
Delos and Delphi, had severally contributed. His worship
was now spread throughout the world, as part of the
conventional religion. The Romans in quite early times
took him over as a great foreign Ἄναξ, just as the Greeks
had taken him from the Lycians. But they breathed
into him nothing of their own spirit ; instead, they
re-named many a Celtic and Iberian god by his name.
Augustus happened to win his decisive victory at Actium
near to a temple of Apollo. He therefore adopted Apollo
as his personal patron, and the talented poets of his

court glorified this act of conventional religiosity by ideas and images borrowed from ancient Greece. There is no inner life in all that. Let us leave the wider world and fix our attention upon Delphi, in order to pierce through seeming to reality. It was an empty phrase when war was declared against the Phocians in the fourth century ostensibly on behalf of the god. True, he performed an epiphany when he scared away the Gauls under Brennus, and to the simpler sort of Aetolian this may have been the genuine miracle which the official world declared it. Two centuries later a Thracian tribe plundered the sanctuary and burnt the temple ; and the world took so little notice that until a few years ago the very fact was forgotten. So small in importance was the Delphi of Cicero's time ! When Nero, the matricide, shrank from entering Delphi, he feared the vengeance of a god ; but it was only the god in his own conscience. The Delphian god had, as a matter of fact, given sanctuary to Orestes and Alcmaeon. A little later we find the gentle and pious Plutarch a priest at Delphi, busily striving by theological speculation to reconcile local rites and legends with his own Platonic philosophy. Unsatisfying as such attempts always seem to us, there is quite often profound thought underlying them. Classical learning has as yet scarcely begun the task of tracing out Greek theology as such. But nothing shows us more clearly how dead the gods really were, than the writers who are trying earnestly to believe in them. This belief was, strictly speaking, stronger among the Christians. To them Apollo was a real devil, whose temple they destroyed ; yet in the oracles which they forged in his name, he confesses his own helplessness against . the new gods.

The temples fell. But in poems and declamations

Phoebus Apollo still maintained a shadowy existence, as the Sun, as the god of poets and musicians, and as the hero of countless idle tales through century after century. At last came our own scientific history. Slowly and laboriously it has learnt to distinguish this god of metaphor and fiction, or even of theology, from that other Apollo to whom the Greeks prayed in the days of living faith. But for too long a time Science was seeking for a formula which should express the whole being of the god—if possible through the etymology of his name. Historical reflection has taught us a different lesson. The gods, too, have their history. Inasmuch as they live only in man's emotions, with those emotions they shift and change ; and it is these that our historical research must follow. We have to understand not one Apollo, but many and diverse Apollos, living and changing in the ritual and belief of diverse places and periods. The cheating and hypocrisy must be as plain before us as the honest credulity and the efforts of theological compromise.

And, when all is said, this is but a preparatory stage, indispensable but only preparatory. For religious emotion and intellectual perception are incommensurables. We must go further. That emotion which inspired the hearts of men long dead must live again in our hearts. We must feel with them that awe and that rapture whose source they worshipped in their gods. We must learn to believe as they believed. Be it in the quiet of our chamber, when we read the verses of some religious poet, be it on the floor of some ancient temple which to the historical sense still preserves its sanctity, we must feel in our own lives the epiphany of the god.

ὠπόλλων οὐ παντὶ φαείνεται, ἀλλ' ὅτις ἐσθλός·
ὅς μιν ἴδηι, μέγας οὗτος· ὃς οὐκ ἴδε, λιτὸς ἐκεῖνος·
ὀψόμεθ', ὦ Ἑκάεργε, καὶ ἐσσόμεθ' οὔποτε λιτοί.